Yale Language Series

LEARN TO WRITE
CHINESE CHARACTERS

Johan Björkstén

Yale University Press   New Haven and London

The original title, "Lär dig skriva kinesiska tecken," was published by Studentlitteratur, Lund, Sweden, 1992. Copyright © Johan Björkstén and Studentlitteratur, Lund, Sweden, 1992.

Designed by Deborah Dutton.

Set in Sabon and Gill Sans Condensed type by The Composing Room of Michigan, Inc., Grand Rapids, Michigan.

Printed in the United States of America by Edwards Brothers, Inc., Ann Arbor, Michigan.

Library of Congress Cataloging-in-Publication Data

Björkstén, Johan, 1964—

    [Lär dig skriva kinesiska tecken. English]

    Learn to write Chinese characters / Johan Björkstén.

       p.   cm.

    Includes bibliographical references and index.

    ISBN 0-300-05771-7 (alk. paper)

    1. Chinese characters. 2. Chinese language—Writing. I. Title.

PL1171.B5613   1994

495.1′82421—dc20   93-41542

                                     CIP

A catalogue record for this book is available from the British Library.

The paper in this book meets the guidelines for permanence and durability of the Committee on Production Guidelines for Book Longevity of the Council on Library Resources.

10 9 8 7 6 5 4

To Cecilia

良師諍友

CONTENTS

ACKNOWLEDGMENTS

The model characters were written by Yan Ruimin, keen pedagogue and expert on fountain pen calligraphy. I am grateful for all the late nights on which he shared his expertise with this Swedish novice, as well as for his patience with my incessant changes in the manuscript and the resulting new calligraphic work.

Cecilia Lindqvist spotted uncountable errors in drafts of the manuscript and contributed many ideas on the teaching of characters. Without her generous help this book would not exist in its present form.

I would also like to thank Qing Yang for providing the drawings for figures 18 and 19, Jonas Arnqvist for his aid with the word processing and review of the text, Jussi Karlgren for his usual enthusiasm and comments on style, and Johan "It-is-totally-unnecessary-to-practice-characters" Nilsson for innumerable opportunities to hone the pro-calligraphy arguments (and for his thorough language editing and help with the original layout), as well as Maarten de Château, Magnus Fiskesjö, Kjell Fornander, Göran Leijonhufvud, and Li Congjia for reading and commenting on the material. David Pankenier provided many valuable suggestions, especially on the English technical terms. My warm thanks to Terry Wolkerstorfer for his thorough review of my English. Finally, I would like to thank the professionals at Yale University Press, especially my editor, Mary Pasti, whose painstaking and enthusiastic work has made this wonderful English edition possible.

INTRODUCTION

Even though characters are one of the most fascinating aspects of the Chinese language, most of us who study Chinese aren't very good at writing them. Translators and scholars who know the language well sometimes have embarrassingly sloppy handwriting. It is a pity that the art of writing has been so little stressed in the teaching of the language. Not only is writing beautiful characters fun, but good handwriting is of much greater importance in learning Chinese than in learning a Western language. There are several reasons for this.

- The characters may seem chaotic to the novice, but their structure is not at all haphazard. Over the millennia they have developed from easily recognizable pictures of objects to highly stylized symbols of script. In the course of this development they have also been standardized to facilitate speed and comfort in writing. Not only must the strokes that make up each character be written in a certain rigidly specified order; they must also be written in a special way, which we will deal with in this book. The technique of writing is thus closely linked to the structure of the characters. By focusing on good handwriting, learners more quickly acquire a feeling for the logic of the Chinese characters, making them easier to remember. Schoolteachers in China pay great attention to the subject of writing.

- Most handwritten characters (in letters and on menus and shop signs, for example) are written in cursive script, where the separate strokes are linked for quick writing. Such characters are much harder to read than the printed forms that beginners learn. Because they are shorthand versions derived from the same roots as the standard forms, the way they are written is closely linked to the way standard characters are written. In developing correct handwriting, you will gain a natural feel for the characters that makes them easier to decipher, even when they are in the cursive style. Actually, it is almost impossible for someone who lacks an adequate foundation in the art of writing to interpret cursive characters.

- For anyone who wants to learn how to write cursive script, reasonable proficiency in standard characters is absolutely essential.

- Calligraphy, the art of writing, is considered in China the noblest of the fine arts. At a very early stage in history it became an abstract and expressionist art form, where meaning is of secondary importance and aesthetic expression the prime concern. Many Chinese hold that calligraphy prolongs the writers' lives, sharpens their senses, and enhances their general well-being. By practicing calligraphy you can achieve a glimpse into Chinese aesthetics and philosophy and learn to appreciate an abstract art form.

There are two principal ways to learn calligraphy. You can begin in the traditional way, with a brush. This calls for long practice, infinite patience, and a good teacher. By practicing with a brush you emphasize the artistic rather than the practical, for few modern Chinese use the brush in everyday life. Good teachers of traditional calligraphy are a rare breed outside Chinese communities.

Your other option is to practice with a fountain pen. This has many advantages. The fountain pen is the writing tool used in present-day China, so you have a practical use for what you learn. The fountain pen is easier to use than the soft, pliable brush, so you can avoid spending time on technique and concentrate on writing neat characters. The principles for writing with a fountain pen hold equally well for pencil and ballpoint pen, though it is easier to form pleasing strokes with a fountain pen. Lastly, you can make do without a teacher. Fountain pens are readily available, and ordinary paper can be used. For brush calligraphy, special Chinese writing paper is preferable.

Many teachers of Chinese hold the misconception that in learning calligraphy it is necessary to start practicing with a brush. As a result, many schools give makeshift courses in brush calligraphy or, more commonly, offer hardly any instruction in the subject at all. In fact, fountain pen calligraphy is becoming more and more popular in the whole Chinese-speaking world; there are many books offering model characters and aesthetic guidance, as well as regular exhibitions and competitions. Practicing with a pen is as good a way to learn the characters as practicing with a brush.

What I address in this book, then, is fountain pen calligraphy, or "calligraphy of the hard pen." To understand and appreciate characters requires some historical background and a simple analysis of the structure and aesthetics of the script. Much has been written on these subjects, and at the end of the book I list a few titles of further interest. On the other hand, there is, as far as I know, no introduction to writing characters with a pen that is designed for a non-Chinese-speaking audience. I hope this book will fill the gap. The material should be well suited for all learners of Chinese, from high school students and first-year undergraduates to old hands who would like to improve their writing technique. Because the book presupposes no previous knowledge of Chinese, it should also attract anyone with an interest in the language and culture of China.

I hope that by following the suggestions made in this book you will be able to learn Chinese characters more easily, deepen your appreciation of their beauty, and have as much fun practicing them as I have had.

THE HISTORY AND STRUCTURE

OF CHARACTERS

Chinese characters constitute one of the oldest forms of writing in the world. Archaeologists making excavations since the 1970s have discovered that characters were already in use in the Stone Age, even though the symbols can probably not be considered script in the true sense of the word. When scholars consider the early history of the characters, they often focus on the **Shāng** dynasty (sixteenth–eleventh centuries B.C.) because of the rich historical material from the period.

Since the sixth century A.D., old pieces of bone, called *dragon bones,* reputedly possessed of beneficial medical powers, have been sold in pharmacies in northern China. In 1899 a Beijing scientist noticed that the bones had inscriptions; and when the symbols were investigated, some could be interpreted as ancient forms of modern Chinese characters. An example of the writing can be seen in figure 1. Their place of origin turned out to be the remains of a **Shāng**-dynasty capital, and its excavation some thirty years after the discovery yielded tens of thousands of the inscribed dragon bones.

The bones are the remains of **Shāng** soothsayers' archives. The **Shāng** people collected turtle shells or shoulder blades from oxen, drilled shallow holes at certain points, and stuck red-hot bronze rods into the indentations. The resulting cracks in the shells and bones were interpreted by the court soothsayers. The prophecies were carved beside the cracks, and the bones were filed in vast archives in the capital. The characters on the bones are called oracle bone characters. Their uniformity and the wide vocabulary employed

Fig. 1. Turtle shell with oracle bone characters

suggest that even three thousand years ago they may already have had a long history. About one-third of the oracle bone characters in the archives have been deciphered.

The structure of the oracle bone characters shows that they are forerunners of modern Chinese script. The characters originated in a number of ways.

- *Pictographs.* From the illustrations in figure 2, we see that some characters were originally pictures. On the left are the oracle bone characters and on the right their modern equivalents. The "primitive" characters on the left were one stage in a long process during which the original pictographs became symbols of script.

- *Characters depicting abstract concepts.* The interpretation of **shàng, xià,** and **bìng** in figure 3 is straightforward. **Hǎo,** *good,* is a picture of a woman holding a child.

mén, *door*

shuǐ, *water*

rì, *sun*

yuè, *moon*

yáng, *sheep*

Fig. 2

shàng, *up; above*

xià, *down*

bìng, *side by side*

hǎo, *good*

Fig. 3

- *Characters formed from a phonetic and a radical.* When the need arose for a character whose meaning was difficult to illustrate with simple pictures, the character was often created by borrowing an existing character with the same pronunciation. To this "pronunciation part" (the phonetic) was added a "meaning marker" (the radical) in order to distinguish the new character from the old one. Take, for example, the character **cǎo**, *grass*. It consists of two parts: a phonetic, **zǎo**, which means *early* but was merely borrowed to hint at the pronunciation of the character, and a radical that means *plant*. The character for *river,* **hé**, is made from the *water* radical and a phonetic pronounced **kě**. If we used characters in English, we might imagine the character for "to read" being made up of a reed symbol (for pronunciation) and the eye radical (to indicate which homophone was intended). The borrowing took place long ago, and sometimes the phonetic is no longer pronounced in exactly the same way as the character that it is part of. Here we have to accept that the pronunciations were once the same. Over 95 percent of all Chinese characters have been formed in this fashion. Figure 4 illustrates two more cases.

- *Characters borrowed without adding a radical.* When a new character was needed, sometimes an old, even obsolete character was invested with the new meaning. The character **lái**, for example, originally meant *a kind of wheat,* but because of its pronunciation it was borrowed as the character for the word *to come:*

Oracle bones are not our only clues to the origins of characters. Another source of knowledge is inscriptions on bronze vessels used for sacrifices and other rituals. Despite the abundant material, however, the origins of many characters remain unclear. Only a small number of characters have had their heritage unequivocally elucidated.

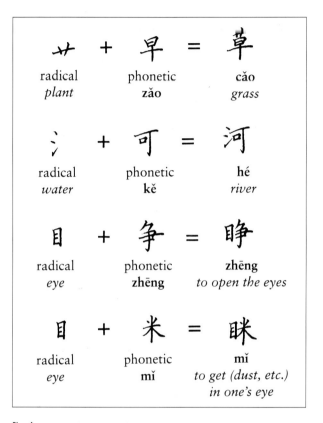

Fig. 4

In older times there was no standardized way of writing, and the same character would appear in any number of variants. Later, characters gradually
became more uniform. The changes were determined in part by new writing
materials (brush, silk, paper) and practical considerations (decreasing the
number of strokes to make the characters easier to write), but also by determined efforts of the authorities.

When the emperor of Qin united China in the third century B.C., he standardized the characters and created what is now called the *small seal script*. An
example can be seen in figure 5. This script is a simplified form of the style
that had been in common use earlier, which we call the *great seal script*. The
small seal script is still used in carving the stone seals with which the Chinese

Fig. 5. Seal script. The picture is a rubbing of an inscription made on stone. Wet paper is applied to the stone, and as it dries, it sinks into the depressions created by the carved characters. Ink is applied to the flat surface of the paper, leaving the sunken portions, the characters, white.

stamp scrolls and documents. It retains many features of the script on the ancient oracle bones.

The development of *clerical script* ran parallel with that of seal script. Clerical script was an even more simplified form of writing, employed at first only for unofficial business. Compare figures 5 and 6 to see the difference between the seal and clerical scripts.

Clerical script, too, has remained in use. Under the Ming and Qing dynasties it was often the vehicle of erotic literature, and nowadays it functions as a variation on the standard characters, much as we might use Gothic type for the Latin alphabet when we wish to be extra fancy.

To write faster than is possible with clerical script, a highly simplified cursive script was developed. In this style, which became known as **cǎoshū,** many separate strokes may be shortened into a single one, and whole parts of a character may be omitted. Strong personal variation makes it hard for the uninitiated to read, as is the case with English shorthand today. **Cǎoshū** is one of the three styles used by modern Chinese in their everyday life. In figure 7 we see a specimen written by **Wáng Xīzhī,** the greatest Chinese calligrapher of all time.

The two other styles commonly used in present-day China are **kǎishū** and **xíngshū. Kǎishū,** or standard script, shown in figure 8, is the most important. It developed in the second century A.D. as a mixture of standardized **cǎoshū** and clerical script. The major features of **kǎishū** are distinctness and legibility—every character has a definite form, and only minor variations are allowed. **Kǎishū** is the model for the printed characters in books, magazines, and newspapers, and it is the style learned by Chinese schoolchildren. Therefore, it is the style that we will practice in this book.

Xíngshū, like **cǎoshū,** is a sort of cursive script that is quicker to write than **kǎishū,** but it is not as extremely personal as **cǎoshū** and is therefore easier to read. An example is given in figure 9. An adult Chinese usually writes in a mixture of **xíngshū** and **cǎoshū,** much as those of us comfortable with a Latin alphabet usually write in cursive script rather than print capitals. Figure 10 compares a few characters written in **kǎishū** (on the left), **xíngshū** (in the middle), and **cǎoshū** (on the right).

Fig. 6. Clerical script (**Hàn** dynasty)

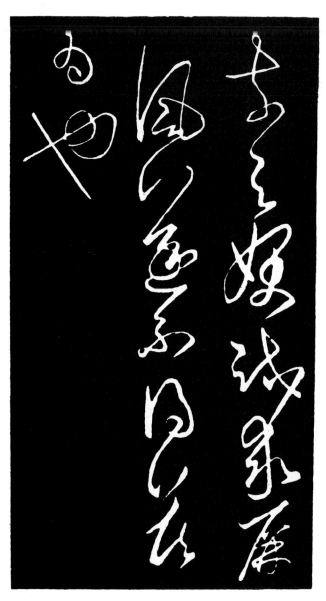

Fig. 7. **Cǎoshū** by **Wáng Xīzhī** (A.D. 321–379)

Fig. 8. **Kǎishū** by **Oūyáng Xún** (A.D. 557–641)

Fig. 9. **Xíngshū** by **Huáng Tíngjiān** (A.D. 1045–1105)

For nearly two thousand years **kǎishū** has, without significant alterations, served as the standard Chinese script. To promote literacy and increase the efficiency of writing, the Chinese Communist regime undertook a script reform in 1956. A new set of simplified characters was set down as the standard for the whole country. This reform was not acknowledged by the Nationalist regime on Taiwan, nor was it carried through in Hong Kong. At present two sets of standard characters are in use worldwide; I will call them *full* and *simplified* characters.

Several principles were used in the simplification of the traditional characters. These are illustrated in figure 11 in the righthand boxes. In certain cases, original antiquated forms were revived as the new standard (*a, b*). In other cases simplified variants from **cǎoshū** were used (*c*), or several strokes were merged into a single one (*d*). Sometimes, simple symbols were substituted for a complex part of a character (*e*) or part of the character was simply deleted (*f, g*). Yet another method was to change the phonetic (*h*). The majority of the "new" characters produced by the reform had already been unofficially used long before.

The simplified characters were much debated, and the controversies continue to this day. The simplified characters are quicker to write, but the simplifica-

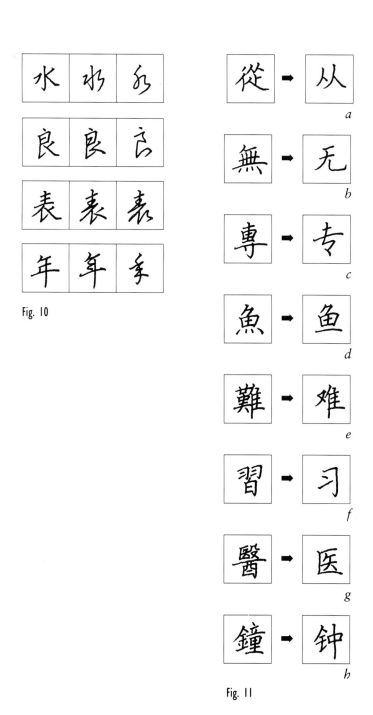

Fig. 10

Fig. 11

tions have made certain characters hard to tell apart. By redoing the characters, the reformers have broken down part of the logic behind their structure.

In the People's Republic of China shop and restaurant signs and publications aimed at overseas Chinese are often written in full characters, whereas almost all books and newspapers are printed with simplified characters. On Taiwan and especially in Hong Kong many of the simplified characters are used in informal communications, but full characters are used in all printed matter. Singapore has taken a middle road by using simplified characters for newspapers and certain books, but full characters still dominate the scene. Unfortunately, this mixed use makes it hard for people who know only one kind of character to get by. Learning to write the full characters takes time and application, but you must be able to recognize them. Not all characters have been simplified. When there are two forms of a character, I use both the full and the simplified forms for the examples and exercises in this book.

Over the years many scholars and politicians have suggested that the Latin alphabet be substituted for the characters, but such a reform has never been tried. There are several reasons.

First of all, the characters are well suited to their purpose. The Chinese language is poor in sounds, and if the Latin alphabet were used, many words would be spelled the same way, making texts difficult to interpret.

Second, the characters are an important unifying factor in a country with many different and mutually incomprehensible spoken dialects. People speak differently but write the same.

Third, Chinese characters are surprisingly practical to use in our modern world. They take a lot of time to learn, but once mastered, they have many advantages. The cursive script is a natural shorthand, which can be used to take notes at a baffling speed. The fax machine circumvents the earlier problems with telexes and telegrams, and Chinese word-processing programs now make it possible to type Chinese more quickly than English. Some people believe that Chinese can be read faster than a language using phonetic script.

Last but not least, the Chinese cherish characters as symbols of their culture and would not willingly see them replaced by any other system of writing.

Looking Up Characters in a Dictionary

As we have just seen, most characters are made up of a *radical,* which gives an approximate meaning, and a *phonetic,* which indicates the pronunciation. When working with a Chinese dictionary, we use the radical to look up the character. Even characters that were historically formed in other ways have been included in this system, making it possible to look them up as well.

We have to recognize the radicals to look up words. Some of the more common ones will be dealt with in a later chapter.

Here is how you look up a character.

First you guess what part the radical is. This is usually easy. Then you count the number of strokes in the radical and look it up in the radical list in the beginning of the dictionary. By the entry for the radical there is a reference to where in the character list the characters with this particular radical can be found. The characters in the character list are arranged according to radical and number of strokes. Count the number of strokes in the rest of the character, not including the radical. When you have found the character in the list, a new reference tells you on what page in the dictionary the entry for the character can be found.

Let us look at an example from a popular dictionary using simplified characters, *A Chinese-English Dictionary* (Beijing: Commercial Press, 1978). We will once again take the character **căo** as an example. It has the following stroke-order:

We immediately suspect that **căo** is under the *plant* radical and we see that this radical contains three strokes. Upon looking in the radical list in the beginning of the dictionary for radicals written with three strokes, we find the *plant* radical: number 50. We count the strokes in the rest of the character **cǎo** and look under number 50 in the character list. As expected, we find **cǎo** under "radical 50—six strokes." By the entry we find a reference to page 66, where we are informed that the character is pronounced **cǎo** and can mean *grass, careless,* or *a sort of cursive Chinese script,* among other things. After the explanations of the character itself we find **cǎo** combined with other characters to form words, such as **cǎomào,** *straw hat,* and **cǎoshū,** *cursive writing.*

THE AESTHETICS OF CHARACTERS:

ALIVE ON PAPER

What makes a Chinese character beautiful? Why do we say that one person writes attractive characters and another ugly ones? Since early times, volume after volume has been written on the techniques and materials of writing, the historical development of characters, and, perhaps more than anything else, the aesthetics of calligraphy. I have divided this topic of aesthetics into two parts, for certain ideals can be appreciated only after learning the basics of writing. But even before you take pen in hand, it is important to discuss how to approach the art of writing.

Let me once more point out, however, that the principal object of this book is to teach you ordinary handwriting, rather than to turn you into an artist. Writing with speed and accuracy is more valuable a skill than making pretty characters. Fortunately, these two objectives tend to merge: the more elegantly you form your characters, the faster you will (eventually) write. When you have learned to appreciate the beauty of the characters, you will also find them easier to memorize.

Figures 12 to 16, along with some earlier examples, indicate the scope and variation of Chinese calligraphy. The elegant characters of Emperor **Huīzōng** in figure 12 conjure up the image of reeds on the shoreline of a quiet lake— the slender strokes bent by the night breeze rustle in the still twilight. Compare this refined atmosphere to the self-conscious, almost rebellious calligraphy in figure 13. The characters in the upper right are bouncing down the paper, possibly on their way to the cocktail party at the bottom of the page.

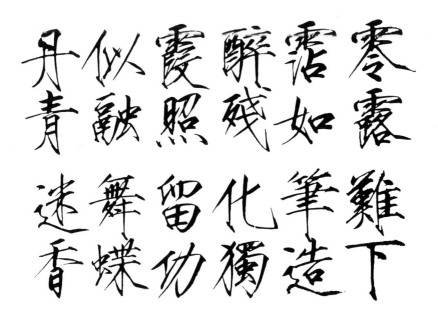

Fig. 12. **Xíngshū** by the **Sòng** emperor **Huīzōng** (twelfth century A.D.)

Fig. 13. **Xíngshū** by **Yán Zhēnqīng** (A.D. 709–785)

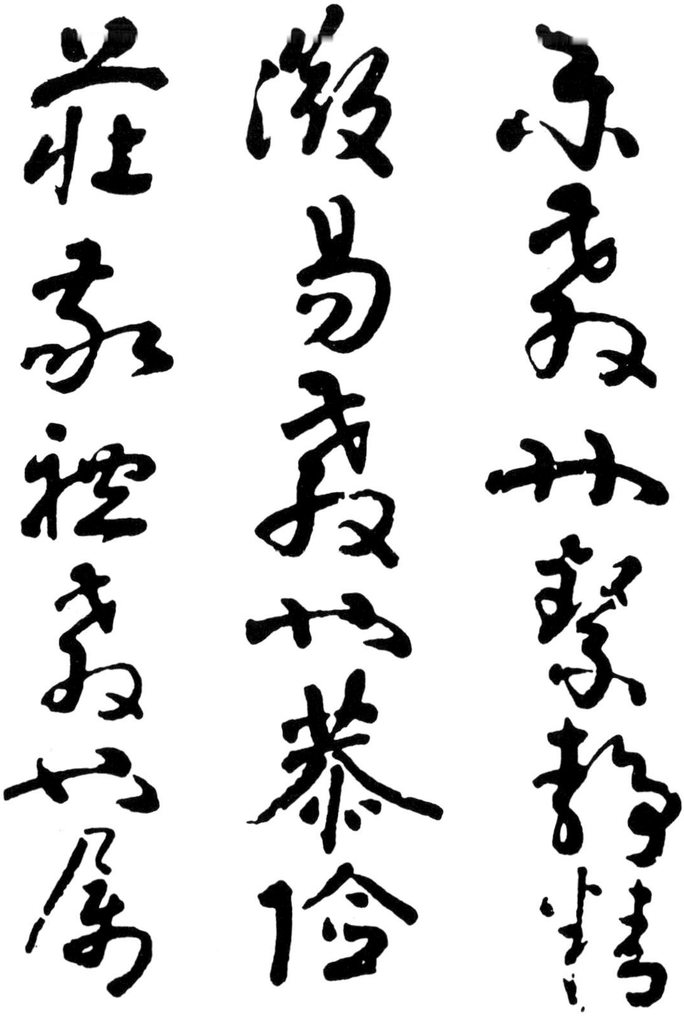

Fig. 14. Anonymous **xíngshū**

Despite superficial differences in the calligraphy of the two artists, their characters are alike in showing life and movement. The **cǎoshū** of **Wáng Xīzhī** in figure 7 evokes the long sweeping sleeves of Chinese folk dancers, whereas **Oūyáng Xún** writes a much more serious hand in figure 8; his **kǎishū** characters are as straight-backed and resolute as the guards at the emperor's palace. The farmers outside, trudging down the street with their heavy burdens, can be found in figure 14. There is a firm, unyielding quality to these characters, as if they were age-old trees, bowed and knotted but with their core wood as strong and resilient as ever. **Sū Shì**'s characters in figure 15 loom menacingly on the paper. They speak about the sudden coming of a thunderstorm—he was clearly inspired by their meaning when he wrote them.

These descriptions may seem overpoetic, but Chinese masters themselves describe their calligraphy this way. The characters are compared to natural phenomena—to trees and cliffs, to waterfalls and storm clouds—to the traits and emotions of human beings, to expressive images that elicit the interest of, and offer inspiration to, the viewer. Characters are described as having an almost musical rhythm, sometimes slow and gentle, sometimes swift and full of energy.

As an abstract art form, calligraphy leaves plenty of room for the viewer's imagination. It is not the likeness to natural objects that matters but rather the feeling of life that permeates the characters. That the characters must be alive is the key to the aesthetics of calligraphy. A Chinese author once wrote this about the spirit of calligraphy: "Every line must be animated; every character must seek the movement of life." Certainly, there is this movement in the calligraphy illustrated here. **Kǎishū**, standard characters, are often called the *standing* style, **xíngshū** the *walking* style, and **cǎoshū** the *running* style—again, movement is emphasized.

A character that has been well executed is in harmony, regardless of whether it is standing still or seems to be going somewhere. It is not about to collapse, it is not stumbling or falling over, but lives its life in equilibrium on the paper. The Chinese dislike rigid symmetry. Instead, the ideal is refined balance, giving the impression that the character has been momentarily frozen in the midst of movement.

Not only have the calligraphers compared their works to nature or to other art forms; they have also sought inspiration there. A famous poem tells how

Fig. 15. **Xíngshū** by **Sū Shì,** also known as **Sū Dōngpō** (A.D. 1037–1101)

Fig. 16. **Căoshū** by **Zhāng Xù** (eighth century A.D.)

Zhāng Xù, a master of calligraphy known for his **căoshū**, saw the famous dancer Gōngsūn do the sword dance:

> Brilliant as **Yì,** the great archer,
> Shooting the nine suns out of the sky,
> Fierce as the onslaught of spirits and dragons
> Wheeling through the heavens,
> She began like a thunderbolt, venting anger,
> Then ended with the glittering calm of rivers and seas.

According to the poet **Dù Fŭ, Zhāng Xù** consummated his **căoshū** after seeing this heavenly performance, being particularly inspired if he had drunk "three glasses of wine"—as **Dù Fŭ** reported—prior to picking up the brush. A specimen of **Zhāng**'s writing can be seen in figure 16.

WRITING CHARACTERS

Having looked at the history and aesthetics of characters, it is high time to start writing. Let's begin by discussing how to practice and then talk about how to form characters that are pleasing to the eye.

The Tools of Writing

The Pen

Use a fountain pen with a round tip. The special pens for calligraphy that are available in the United States, Europe, and elsewhere usually have flat tips and are therefore not suitable for writing Chinese characters. The best pens are the ones whose shaft covers nearly the entire tip, giving it firm support (fig. 17). This is the kind of fountain pen most common in China, and you should be able to find one in a good stationery store in your neighborhood as well.

The Ink

Chinese carbon ink (**tànsù mòshuǐ**) is the ideal choice if you can find it. Shanghai brand is the best. The ink is a deeper black than most inks used

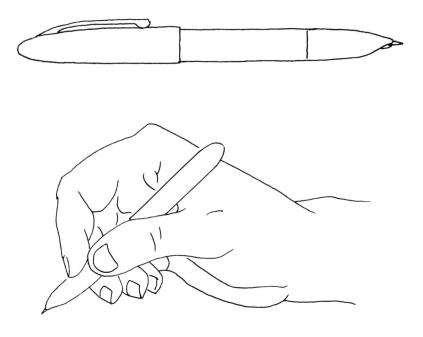

Fig. 17

outside China, in keeping with the Chinese calligraphic tradition of "black characters on white paper." The high contrast makes it easy to spot errors. Also, it is almost waterproof after it dries. If you cannot find carbon ink, use any black ink.

The Paper

The paper should be crosshatched or marked off in squares, with each square big enough to contain a whole character. Squares makes it easier for the beginner to produce characters of uniform size. The paper should be glossy enough that the ink dries with sharp edges and does not run. Never put the paper directly on a hard table when writing—satisfactory strokes are extremely difficult to produce. Instead, put fifteen to twenty layers of soft paper (ideally the tissuelike paper used for wiping camera lenses) under the sheet you are writing on.

How to Practice

The first thing to do with any new character is to carefully memorize the stroke order. Simple rules govern the order in which the strokes that make up a character must be written. We will wait a little before learning these rules, for they require that we know the basic strokes. Still, it is very important to write with the correct stroke order, so pay careful attention to the order in what follows.

The tried and true method for practicing writing is to copy the characters of an accomplished calligrapher. While you are unsure of your technique, you may want to put a thin, transparent sheet of paper over the characters you are copying and trace them with your pen. Once you understand the rudiments, you should copy by first examining the model and then writing your character in exactly the same way. You should *not* look at one stroke at a time, write it, consider the next stroke, write it, and so on. Instead, you should look at the *whole* character, analyze its structure, turn your head away, and not look at the model character again until you have written all the strokes. When you have completed your character, you should compare it with the model, find out what mistakes you made, and try again. This is the only way to fix the picture of the character firmly in your mind and make rapid progress.

The principle behind this method of practicing has its roots deep in the Chinese aesthetic tradition. Chinese artists are expected to see the whole painting with their inner eye before beginning to work; then they simply paint what they see. This approach is called *having a bamboo completed in your chest.* Chinese watercolors and calligraphic works are often executed in a very short time—the creative work is done before the artist touches the brush.

It is taboo to go back and alter a character while writing. If a stroke fails, begin the whole character over again.

Practice only three or four different characters a day, at least to begin with. Otherwise, you do not have time to learn them thoroughly enough, and you grow too tired to analyze what you are doing right and what you are doing wrong. You learn the characters in a sloppy way and do not really improve your writing.

Write each character at least a hundred times.

Save everything you write and date the papers. Just as with all learning, there will be times when you do not feel as though you are making any progress. It can be heartening to look at the characters that you wrote a month or two earlier. You will be surprised at the difference.

Sit correctly at a desk or table that is not too high. You should be able to rest your arms comfortably on the tabletop. Put the paper straight in front of you and do not slant it too much. Many learners slant the paper and bend over when writing. Don't do either when you write in Chinese. Hold the pen between thumb and forefinger, letting it rest gently on your curved middle finger (fig. 17). The tip of the pen should point forward on the paper and should form a forty-five-degree angle with it. Sit back in the chair so the chairback supports your lower back as much as possible. Be as upright as possible without tensing your back and shoulders. (You should sit this way when writing in English as well.)

Try to practice on a daily basis. It is much better to practice for fifteen minutes every day than not to practice for a while and then suddenly sit for hours on end at the writing table.

At the end of this book there are models for a hundred or so of the most common characters. Later you may choose models that you think look good. Copying characters written with a brush is fine, but you must catch the spirit of the characters rather than copying them directly, for a fountain pen can never reproduce the thick strokes of a writing brush.

The Basic Strokes

The standard characters are made up of individual strokes arranged in a certain way. The form of each stroke is very important for the form of the whole character. It is therefore necessary to learn proper basic strokes to write acceptable characters. Once you have spent some time practicing the basic strokes, you will have done half the job of acquiring a good Chinese hand. Those little twists and turns may seem insignificant, but they have not been put there on a whim. Rest assured that over the past few millennia, Chinese calligraphers have developed a method of writing that is practical, quick, and elegant.

Traditionally, calligraphers have recognized eight basic strokes for the characters. These are the strokes appearing in the character **yǒng:**

 yǒng, *eternal*

The eight basic strokes are the following (in traditional order):

Below I present the eight basic strokes and give examples of ways they can be executed. The order in which they appear is not the traditional one—I have chosen to present them in a way that I hope will make them easier for the foreigner to learn. In addition, there are practice characters illustrating each stroke. I suggest that you practice one or two strokes at a time and write a few hundred a day. Do not start a new stroke until you feel comfortable with the one you are working on. If you practice half an hour a day, you should feel reasonably satisfied with your basic strokes in two to three weeks.

Héng

The first stroke is called **héng,** or *horizontal,* and looks like this:

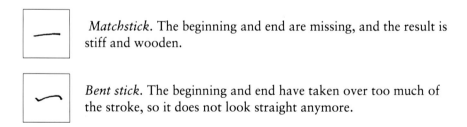

If you look at it carefully, you will notice that it is not a simple straight line. It is not quite horizontal but slants slightly upward, and it is bent without looking crooked, like a flexible twig or a bone.

To write the stroke, set your pen down at the left with a certain force. Then move it slightly downward and to the right. This gives you the little ingress at the left—the well-defined start, separate from the rest of the stroke, like the tensing of muscles before a jump. Execute the stroke itself more quickly, and finish by again pressing more firmly and moving the pen slightly down and to the right. It will feel very awkward to write so carefully, but your speed will soon increase.

Avoid the following mistakes:

Matchstick. The beginning and end are missing, and the result is stiff and wooden.

Bent stick. The beginning and end have taken over too much of the stroke, so it does not look straight anymore.

Here are some exercises. Note the stroke order!

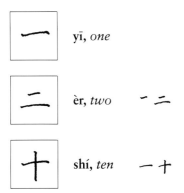

yī, *one*

èr, *two*

shí, *ten*

Héng is rather hard to write. If you feel frustrated, try the next stroke for a while and then return to **héng.**

Shù 竖

The second stroke is called **shù,** meaning *vertical,* and comes in two variants, *dropping dew* and *suspended needle:*

When writing, you begin these two variants in the same way. Put the pen down with a certain force, move it slightly downward and to the right, and then write the stroke itself with a somewhat quicker movement, exerting only moderate pressure on the pen. Whereas the **héng** stroke slants gently upward rather than being perfectly horizontal, **shù** should be absolutely vertical. You finish *dropping dew* by moving the pen with a constant pressure to the end of the stroke and calmly lifting it from the paper. At the very end, you may even move the pen backward for half a millimeter or so. This gives the feeling that the stroke has been executed with careful control and not just tossed down.

34

To finish the *suspended needle*, start slowly decreasing the pressure about two-thirds of the way down the stroke, and continue decreasing it until the pen leaves the paper.

Avoid the following mistakes:

Nail's head. The beginning is overdone.

Rat's tail. This is crooked and lacking in power. You have not given the stroke itself enough energy.

Hemp thread. This stroke begins narrowing too soon and looks as though it is about to break in two. Keep applying pressure all the way down to the tip, and do not let the stroke taper off until you are a millimeter or two from the end.

Dropping dew is used when the **shù** stroke meets another stroke at the top or bottom, and the *suspended needle* is used when **shù** passes through the whole character like a skewer. This is evident in the following exercises:

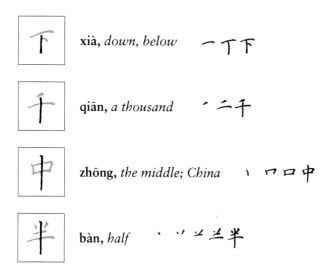

xià, *down, below*

qiān, *a thousand*

zhōng, *the middle; China*

bàn, *half*

Piě

The third basic stroke is called **piě** and functions as a "left leg" in many characters. It should look like the tusk of an elephant:

Piě is comparatively easy to write well. The ingress is about the same as for **shù,** but you must avoid the mistake of curving the stroke too much:

 Archer's bow. This stroke is too bent, and there is no difference between beginning and end.

Here are some exercises in writing **piě:**

 rén, *man, person*   丿 人

huǒ, *fire*   丶 丷 少 火

Nà   捺

The fourth basic stroke is called **nà.** It is rather hard to write. If **piě** is the left leg, then **nà** is the right leg:

Here is how **nà** looks in the character **dà,** *big:*

Note how **nà** conveys the impression of a leg with a foot at the end and how this leg stabilizes the character.

To write **nà,** you should feel in the beginning as if you are striving upward and to the right, even though the stroke slopes downward the whole time. At the start of the "foot," press a little harder with the pen and at the same time change direction to achieve a clear but gentle "joint" in the stroke.

Avoid the following mistakes:

 Hockey stick. The end is crooked and sticks up.

 The foot is too marked, so the stroke looks broken.

 Sagging rope. The stroke does not strive upward at the beginning; it looks feeble.

Here are some exercises:

 mù, *tree; wood*

 jìn, *close, nearby*

shì, *to be* 丶 冂 冂 日 旦 早 早 昰 是

Tiǎo 挑

Tiǎo must be carefully differentiated from **piě**, which has a similar shape but is written in the opposite direction. **Tiǎo** is a variant of **héng**, so it is written from left to right:

Here are some exercises:

 dǎ, *to beat, to hit* 一 亅 扌 扩 打

 hóng, *red* (full form) 乙 幺 幺 爹 爹 糸 糹 紅 紅

 hóng, *red* (simplified form) 乙 幺 纟 纟 红 红

 pǎo, *to run, to move fast* 丶 冂 口 甲 甲 呈 足 趵 趵 跑 跑

Diǎn 点

The sixth basic stroke is **diǎn,** the *dot.* Although making a dot may sound easy, this stroke is one of the hardest to master. It is crucial to the harmony of the whole character. The dot can be written in a number of ways, but three basic types can be distinguished. The first looks like a short **tiǎo:**

The second resembles a **piě:**

The last is a real dot and should look like an elongated apple seed:

Sometimes the dot can be very long:

Dots often occur in groups, and each dot in the group should be unique, so that the whole does not look dull and repetitive. A few exercises follow.

xué, *to study,* *to learn* (full form)　ʼ ʾ ʿ ʾ ʿ ʿ ʾ ʿ ʿ ʿ ʿ ʿ ʿ 與 學 學 學

 xué, *to study, to learn* (simplified form)　丶 丷 丷 丷 兴 学 学 学

 hé, *river*　丶 冫 冫 冫 氵 沔 沔 沔 河

 wén, *language; literature*　丶 亠 亅 文

 mǐ, *rice*　丶 丷 丷 半 半 米

 diǎn, *dot* (full form)　丶 冂 冂 冃 四 四 甲 里 黑 黑 黑 黑 黑 點 點 點 點

 diǎn, *dot* (simplified form)　丶 卜 卜 占 占 占 点 点 点

 hēi, *black*　丶 冂 冂 冃 四 四 甲 里 黑 黑 黑 黑

Gōu 钩

The seventh basic stroke is **gōu,** the *hook.* Gōu comes in four variants. The first begins like a **shù,** but you finish it by moving the pen slightly downward and to the left, after which you lift it from the paper while moving it diagonally upward to the left. The stroke thus acquires a little "heel" to stand on:

The second, called the *reclining hook*, should be softly and evenly bent. You finish it by moving the pen backward, toward the center of the character:

The third hook is a more upright form of the reclining hook:

Finally, there is a very common hook that begins as a **héng** and is ended by moving the pen downward to the right and then backward and to the left:

Avoid the following mistakes:

Fish hook. The **shù**, or *vertical,* part is bent and has fused with the heel.

Triangle. The heel is missing.

The tip slants outward; the character will lose its energy and coherence.

This stroke is too curved.

The turn is too pronounced and looks as though it is composed of several short segments rather than a single stroke.

Exercises:

shuǐ, *water*

dài, *generation*

sī, *to think*

zì, *(written) character*

chéng, *to become*

Zhé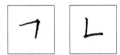

The last stroke to learn is the *bend*, **zhé.** It occurs in two variants, both of which are often used to frame characters:

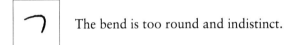

Note that each corner is made with a single stroke.

Avoid the following mistakes:

The bend is too round and indistinct.

The bend seems to have several distinct segments; it looks broken and lacks strength.

Exercises:

guó, *country* (full form)

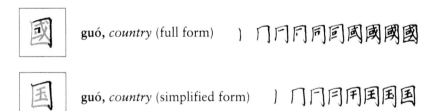

guó, *country* (simplified form)

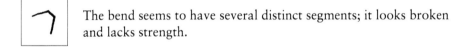

qū, *area* (full form) 一 ナ ア ヂ 丐 品 區

 qū, *area* (simplified form) 一 丁 又 区

Some Composite Strokes

You may have noticed that some strokes that appear to have two separate parts count as a single stroke. These *composite strokes* can be seen as combinations of the eight basic strokes, and it is not really necessary to practice them separately. I include them here as an orientation.

Héngzhé wāngōu 横折弯钩

One of the most common composite strokes is the **héngzhé wāngōu:**

It is easy to see why this stroke is also called the *floating goose hook*. It is used, for example, in the character **jiǔ**, *nine:*

) 九

Shùtiǎo 竖挑

As the name indicates, this stroke comprises a **shù** and a **tiǎo,**

It appears, for example, in the character **mín,** *people:*

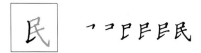

Piězhé 撇折

Another very common composite stroke is **piězhé:**

It is the first stroke in the character **nǚ**, *woman:*

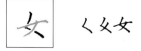

Héngzhé wānpiě   横折弯撇

This stroke

is used, for example, in the character **jí,** *to reach, to attain:*

Héngzhé shùtiǎo   横折竖挑

This stroke

is the larger part of the simplified form of the very common radical meaning *word,* here in the character **shuō,** *to say, to speak:*

 (simplified form)

 (full form)

Stroke Order

There is only one more thing to consider before we can write freely: stroke order. Sample characters are given to illustrate the eight rules to follow. If you practice the characters, you will soon learn the rules intuitively and not have to think about them as you write. Below, only simplified characters are used as examples of the rules.

Rule 1. **Héng** comes before **shù**; that is, horizontal strokes come before vertical ones:

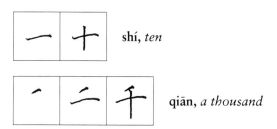

shí, *ten*

qiān, *a thousand*

When a **héng** forms the bottom of a character, it is written last:

wáng, *king*

Rule 2. **Piě** comes before **nà**; that is, a left leg comes before a right one:

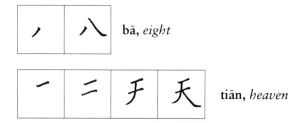

bā, *eight*

tiān, *heaven*

Rule 3. Characters are written from top to bottom:

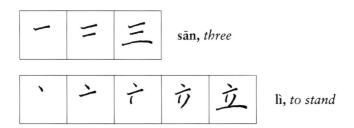

sān, *three*

lì, *to stand*

Rule 4. Characters are written from left to right:

dì, *the ground; place*

hǎo, *good*

Rule 5. If the character is framed from above, the frame is written first:

jù, *sentence*

tóng, *same*

Rule 6. If the character is framed from below, the frame is written last:

hán, *letter, epistle*

Rule 7. Frames are closed last:

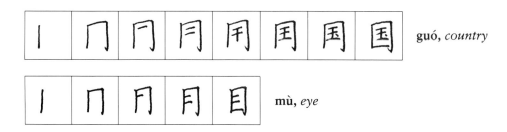

guó, *country*

mù, *eye*

Rule 8. In symmetrical characters the middle is written first, then the sides:

shuǐ, *water*

xiǎo, *small*

These rules do not unequivocally cover all situations. When no rule seems applicable, you must simply learn the stroke order by heart. If you are conscientious about this from the start, you will quickly develop a feeling for what is correct. Sometimes the official stroke order is changed by calligraphers to make the character easier to write. Such changes in stroke order are not made lightly. They are indeed very rare and are most often based on stroke orders from other styles than **kǎishū**. One example is the character **bì**, *must,* which should, by the above rules, be written from left to right:

This is the official stroke order, but if you write it this way, the components are very hard to balance well. If you write it with the **cǎoshū** stroke order, however, the composition becomes much more harmonious:

Another example is **fāng,** *place, location,* which can be written in the following two ways. The first way is the official way, but the second way makes it easier to produce a well-balanced character.

THE AESTHETICS OF CHARACTERS:

COMPOSITION

In the first chapter on aesthetics we discussed the characters from a general artistic perspective and learned to see them in the "right" way. Here we will concentrate on how to *write* good-looking characters.

There are a number of handy guidelines to arranging the parts of a character in the most appealing way. By and large, they have been valid for two thousand years, but they were formulated most clearly by the fifteenth-century calligrapher **Lǐ Chūn**. We will look at a modern analysis of some of his basic principles of composition.

Some Characters Have a Key Stroke

In many characters there is a key stroke on which the whole structure depends. This stroke must be executed to give a vigorous and harmonious impression. In **zhì**, *to arrive, to attain,* the bottom **héng** stroke carries the weight of the whole character and must therefore be firm and stable:

The long hook in the middle of **xīn,** *heart,* sweeps out to make the character cohere. If the hook is badly written, the other strokes look like lost cotton wads tossed by the wind:

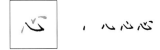

This is also true in **shèng,** *flowering, flourishing,* where the other strokes seem to lean on the long elegant hook:

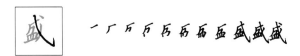

The upper right part of **dào,** *path; way,* rests on the long **nà** stroke at the bottom:

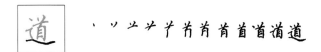

In **qīng,** *clear,* the three dots—depicting water droplets—tie the character together. Note how the uppermost dot strives inward and down while the bottom one strives upward:

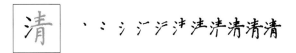

When the key stroke forms the center of the character, as the **shù** stroke does in **zhōng**, *middle; China,* it becomes especially clear. The stroke must stand absolutely straight to give the character balance:

Characters Fit in Imaginary Squares

Chinese characters are basically square. The sample characters in the earlier parts of the book have all been written in red squares, and this is how they are traditionally presented in order to make them easy to analyze and copy. Some characters are tall and skinny, others are broad and squashed, but as far as possible characters are made to conform to a square pattern. To achieve this, the various parts of the character are written in different ways, depending on where they appear in the whole.

Look, for example, at the character **chē**, *wagon, cart:*

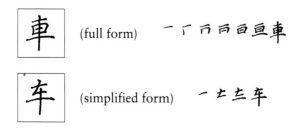

When **chē** stands on its own as a character, it is given ample space horizontally to fill its square, but when it plays the role of the radical in the character **liàng**, *vehicle,* it is elongated to make room for the righthand part of the character:

(simplified form)

The bottom **héng** stroke has been shortened and is written as a **tiǎo** stroke to avoid poking the right part in the ribs.

Another example of how the parts adapt to fit the whole is the character **lín,** *forest:*

Lín is composed of two *trees* (**mù**):

If both trees were written in the same way, the strokes would cross in the middle:

This looks messy and would make the character harder to read. Therefore, the **nà** stroke forming the right leg of the first tree has been changed into **diǎn,** a dot, to make room for the second tree. For similar reasons, **piě** and **nà** are written as dots in many other characters, too.

When you write, the imagined squares around the characters should always be the same size, regardless of how many strokes the character contains. Complex characters must be written with small, light strokes in order not to become swollen and clumsy.

Characters that have a frame often create a massive impression and must be written smaller than others in order not to *seem* too large. Examples are

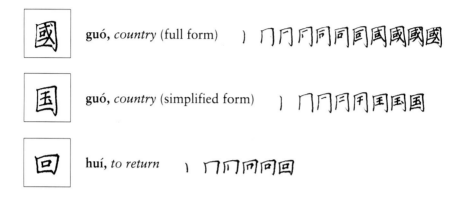

guó, *country* (full form)

guó, *country* (simplified form)

huí, *to return*

Repeated Elements Are Executed with Variation

The character **lín,** *forest,* also illustrates another important principle: avoid stiff symmetry and lifeless repetition. If the same element occurs several times in one character, you should try to make each occurrence different from the others. Other clear examples are characters in which several **héng** strokes are stacked:

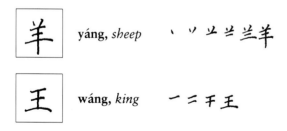

yáng, *sheep*

wáng, *king*

Note how the horizontal strokes are written with different lengths, so that the whole is harmonious without being rigid and boring. The topmost **héng** seems to strive upward, the bottommost downward. On the other hand, the strokes must be evenly spaced; otherwise, the result is not so attractive:

The king on the left looks as if he has swallowed something too big, and the right one's trousers have fallen down.

Some Characters Have Left and Right Parts

Many characters can be seen as having a left-right structure, a left-middle-right structure, a top-bottom structure, or a top-middle-bottom structure, depending on the elements of which they are composed. By dividing characters into these groups, we can find some general rules that will help us distribute the parts of each character harmoniously within the square in which it is written.

We have already seen how the two trees in **lín** have to accommodate each other to produce a forest. The world of the characters is, however, not equal. Certain elements that appear in characters always yield to others. We might say that they are intrinsically small. The following are all examples of such elements:

Most of them are radicals, and their meanings are dealt with in the chapter about radicals.

How to treat these small pieces in the composition of a character can be summarized thus: If the small part is on the left, it should strive upward; if it is on the right, it should strive downward. The following characters illustrate the first part of this rule:

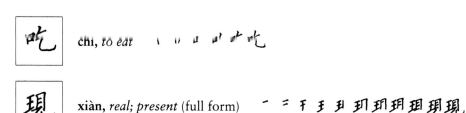

If the small elements on the lefthand side were placed farther down in the character, the result would be clumsy:

The second part of the rule can be illustrated with the characters **zhī** and **hóng**:

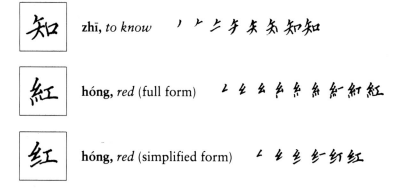

The counterexamples show what happens when the small parts on the right-hand side are placed too high up in the character:

Just as there are intrinsically small elements, there are intrinsically long ones. These include the following:

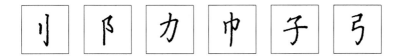

When these appear in characters with a left-right structure, they must always be given ample room to stretch out.

Some Characters Have Left, Middle, and Right Parts

To fit into the square pattern, the elements of broad, three-part characters must be as elongated as possible. Intrinsically long elements are easy to place, and if they appear in the middle they are usually made to be the longest part of the character. Small parts can be harder to fit in. When the small part is on one side of the character, the general rule still applies—small parts on the left strive upward; small parts on the right strive downward. When a small part is in the middle, it usually strives upward as well:

bān, *class in school; work shift*

shù, *tree* (full form)

shù, *tree* (simplified form) 一 十 十 才 木 朽 权 权 树 树

 jiē, *street* ' ' 彳 彳 彳 彳 彳 彳 彳 街 街

 一 十 十 廿 艹 艹 节 芦 芦 董 荳 荳 菫 萋 萋 萋 萋 難

nán, *difficult* (full form)

 nán, *difficult* (simplified form) ' 又 ㄨ 叉 叉 叉 难 难 难 难

Some Characters Have a Top-Bottom Structure

In characters that contain top and bottom parts, and especially in those that contain three parts—top, middle, and bottom—the parts must be flattened to give the character as compact a look as possible. A good example is the character xǐ:

 xǐ, *happiness* 一 十 士 士 吉 吉 吉 吉 吉 喜 喜 喜

If the individual parts are too elongated, the character becomes ridiculously tall:

Framed Characters

We have dealt with characters that are written with a frame around them. Many characters are only partially framed, however, and they can be divided into four subgroups: those framed from the left, those framed from the right, those framed from above, and those framed from below. The most useful general rules are for characters framed from the right or from above. In characters framed from the right, the contents should snuggle up to the upper righthand corner of the frame:

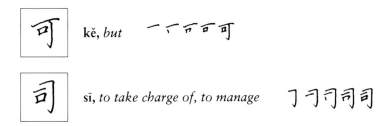

kě, *but*

sī, *to take charge of, to manage*

In characters framed from above, the contents should strive upward, leaving an empty space in the lower part of the frame:

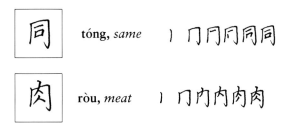

tóng, *same*

ròu, *meat*

A Few Difficult Characters

Let us finish by looking at some particularly interesting characters in detail. A few are hard to master, so we will pay special attention to them.

As we have seen, sometimes the strokes keep a character together and focus its energy inward. Consider the grammatical particle ér. You can see how the shù stroke on the left and the hook on the right strive toward the center:

 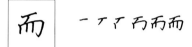

If this feeling is lost, the results are catastrophic:

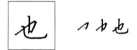

The character yě, *too,* is very hard to write well:

Because yě is very common, you should invest some time in mastering it. First, note how slanted the long héng part of the upper hook is; the typeset character has a horizontal héng, but if it is handwritten that way, the character looks awkward:

Second, the three shù strokes should be evenly spaced to avoid the following ugly result:

The characters **bù,** *no,* and **wù,** *prohibited, don't,* teeter on a thin, pointed base and therefore need to have a poised and elegant upper part to help them retain their balance:

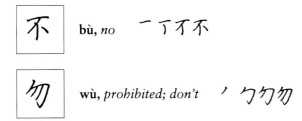

The fewer strokes a character contains, the harder it is to write. This general observation applies to **rù,** *to enter, to go in,* and **rén,** *man, human,* both of which depend on the fresh vigor of the **nà,** the right leg:

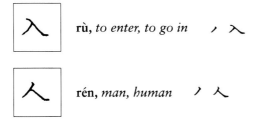

The character **mŭ,** *mother,* is written with a somewhat unusual stroke order. Note how the framework slants. If the character is written with straight angles, it loses life.

Finally, let us look at the character **nŭ,** *woman.* The long **héng** stroke must rest firmly on the two crossed legs, and the **shù,** or vertical, part of the first stroke should determine the central axis of the character:

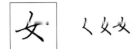

Well executed, this is an elegant character, but it needs to be only slightly off balance to lose its beauty. It illustrates how dependent characters are on the interplay and fine-tuned equilibrium of the various strokes and therefore makes a good ending to our discussion of the aesthetics of the characters.

THE RADICALS

In the history chapter we saw that characters are composed of a radical and a phonetic and that this is the basis for how they are classified in dictionaries. Some radicals occur very frequently and are well worth a more careful look. Dictionaries use over two hundred different radicals. Below I will present thirty-odd of the most common ones and give examples of characters in which they appear. You should practice the characters until you master the radicals. For certain radicals that tend to be hard to write, I have added detailed instructions on how to overcome the problems.

The name of each radical is given in English and Chinese. You need not learn the Chinese names immediately, but the list will be handy to refer to when you do want to memorize them. Whereas the Chinese names usually have little or nothing to do with the history and development of the characters, the English names are more informative.

For radicals that can be used independently as characters, I have included the pronunciation and meaning of the independent form. Sometimes the usage is a result of the simplification reform and is unrelated to the history of the character. Where the history of the radical is well known and can serve as a mnemonic aid to learning the characters, I touch on it briefly.

The lid radical

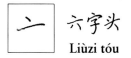 六字头
Liùzi tóu

、　亠　亠六　六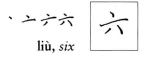
liù, *six*

、　亠　亠产　亠产亠古亠古京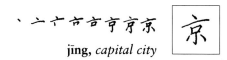
jīng, *capital city*

The cliff radical

 偏厂
Piān chǎng

This radical originally depicted a cliff where people could live, a reference to the cavelike dwellings made in cliffs in some areas of China. The radical is often used in characters for rooms or buildings.

一厂厂厂厂厂厂所所所厣厣厰厰 厰
chǎng, *factory* (full form)

一厂 厂
chǎng, *factory* (simplified form)

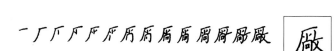

一丁厂厅
tīng, *hall, room* (simplified form)

The roof radical

 宝盖头
Bǎogài tóu

丶丷宀宀宁字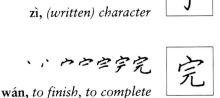
zì, *(written) character*

丶丷宀宀宁字完
wán, *to finish, to complete*

When the whole character contains many strokes, especially when these are **piě** and **nà** strokes, the roof radical must be made rather small. This is, for example, the key to writing the characters **jiā** and **ān** in an aesthetic way. Compare the examples below to **zì** and **wán** above.

丶丷宀宀宁宇宇豖豖家
jiā, *home, family*

丶丷宀宀宀安安
ān, *calm*

The shed radical

广字旁
Guǎngzi páng

This radical originally depicted a side view of a house with no front wall.

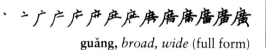

guǎng, *broad, wide* (full form)

guǎng, *broad, wide* (simplified form)

diàn, *shop*

The knife radical

立刀旁
Lì dāo páng

dāo, *knife*

bié, *other; don't*

The man or person radical

立人旁
Lì rén páng

ノ イ 竹 仲 他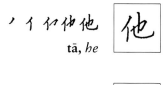
tā, *he*

ノ イ 亻' 亻尔 亻尔 你 你
nǐ, *you*

The left-step radical

彳
双人旁
Shuāng rén páng

ノ ク 彳 彳' 行 行 行
two pronunciations: **xíng,** *to go;* **háng,** *row, line*

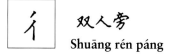
ノ ク 彳 彳 彳日 彳日 很 很 很
hěn, *very, to a high degree*

The ear radical

 双耳旁
Shuāng ěr páng

This radical has two entries in dictionaries, one for when it appears on the left of the character and one for when it appears on the right. The two cases have different historical origins. The left ear radical was originally the character **fù**, which is written thus:

This character is still in use and means *high place, mound*. The right ear radical is a simplified form of the character **yì**, meaning *place where people gather, city*:

The two following characters illustrate the use of both left and right ear radicals. Note that the **shù** stroke of the left ear is written as a *dropping dew* stroke, whereas in the right ear a long *suspended needle* stroke is used in its place.

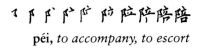

péi, *to accompany, to escort*

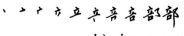

bù, *department*

The three-dots-of-water radical

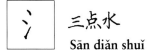 三点水
Sān diǎn shuǐ

` ` ˋ ㇀ 氵 汁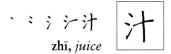
zhī, *juice*

` ˋ ㇀ 氵 氵 沪 沪 沪 淠 淠 湡 湯 湯 湯
tāng, *soup, broth* (full form)

` ˋ ㇀ 氵 汤 汤 汤
tāng, *soup, broth* (simplified form)

The standing heart radical

 竖心旁
Shù xīn páng

` ㇀ 忄 忄 忙 忙
máng, *to be busy, to have a lot to do*

` ㇀ 忄 忄 忄 忄 怕 怕 怕
pà, *to be afraid*

The basic heart radical

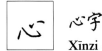
Xīnzi dǐ

The character **xīn,** *heart,* depends on the long hook to hold it together. The three dots, in contrast, should strive outward, lifting the character and lending it volume, to give the impression of a sail filled by the wind. When the heart appears as a radical, it must be flattened to make room for the elements above it, but the dots should not be squeezed in. If they do not strive outward and upward, the whole character will have a deflated appearance:

，㇐心心
xīn, *heart*

ノイ 伫 仲 竹 你 你 您 您 您
nín, *you (polite form)*

，㇐ 刍 刍 刍 刍 急 急 急
jí, *impatient; worried*

The door radical (full form)

門 门字旁
Ménzi páng

ㄱ ㄱ ㅋ ㄸ ㄸ ㄸ 門門門門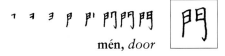
mén, *door*

ㄱ ㄱ ㅋ ㄸ ㄸ ㄸ 門門門門門問問
wèn, *to ask*

The door radical (simplified form)

门 门字旁
Ménzi páng

丶 亻 门
mén, *door*

丶 亻 门问问问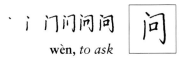
wèn, *to ask*

The walking radical

Zǒuzhī páng

This radical is very difficult to execute correctly. It contains three strokes. You should begin by writing the **diǎn**, or dot. The short **héng** should be connected to a **zhé** ending in a softly curved downward stroke. The final **nà** stroke should give the impression of a soft hill on which the rest of the character can lean.

By all means avoid the common error of breaking the curved downward stroke of the **zhé**:

The zigzag pattern makes the character ugly and lowers your writing speed.

dào, *path; way*

jìn, *to enter, to go in* (full form)

jìn, *to enter, to go in* (simplified form)

The hand radical

 提手旁
Tíshǒu páng

一 十 才 扌 打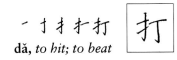
dǎ, *to hit; to beat*

一 十 才 扌 扎 扣 把 把
bǎ, *handle*

The plant radical (full form)

 草字头
Cǎozi tóu

㇄ ㇐ ㇉ ㇉ ㇉ ㇉ ㇉ 花
huā, *flower*

The plant radical (simplified form)

 草字头
Cǎozi tóu

一 十 艹 艹 艹 花 花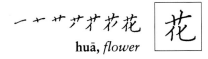
huā, *flower*

The mouth radical

 口字旁
Kǒuzi páng

丶 冂 口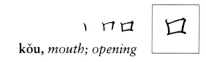
kǒu, *mouth; opening*

丶 冂 口 叻 叫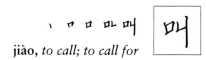
jiào, *to call; to call for*

丶 冂 口 口⁻ 吐 吐
two pronunciations: **tǔ**, *to spit*, and **tù**, *to vomit*

The eating radical (full form)

 食字旁
Shízi páng

丿 人 仐 今 今 仒 仑 食 食 食 食
shí, *to eat*

丿 𠂆 𠂉 今 今 仒 仑 食 食 飠 飮 飰 飯 飯
fàn, *rice; food*

丿 𠂆 𠂉 今 今 仒 仑 食 食 飠 飲 飲 飲
yǐn, *beverage*

The eating radical (simplified form)

食字旁
Shízi páng

丿 𠂊 饣 饣 饣 饭 饭 饭
fàn, *rice; food*

丿 𠂊 饣 饣 饣 饮 饮 饮
yǐn, *beverage*

The woman radical

女字旁
Nǚzi páng

𡿨 𡿨 女 女
nǚ, *woman*

𡿨 𡿨 女 女 女 妇 妇 妈 妈 媽 媽 媽
mā, *mother* (full form)

𡿨 𡿨 女 妇 妈 妈
mā, *mother* (simplified form)

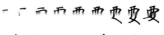

yào, *to want; to be going to*

The silk radical (full form)

绞丝旁

Jiǎosī páng

xiàn, *thread*

The silk radical (simplified form)

绞丝旁

Jiǎosī páng

xiàn, *thread*

The word radical (full form)

言字旁
Yánzi páng

丶 一 亠 言 言 言 言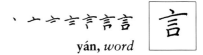
yán, *word*

丶 一 亠 言 言 言 訂 訂 詞 詞 詞 詞
cí, *word*

丶 一 亠 言 言 言 言 訂 訶 評 評 語 語
yǔ, *language*

The word radical (simplified form)

言字旁
Yánzi páng

丶 讠 订 词 词 词 词
cí, *word*

丶 讠 讠 订 讨 语 语 语 语
yǔ, *language*

The horse radical (full form)

馬 马字旁
Mǎzi páng

一 二 三 手 馬 馬 馬 馬 馬   馬

mǎ, *horse*

丶 冂 冖 冖 罒 罒 罒 罒 罵 罵 罵 罵 罵   罵

mà, *to scold*

The horse radical (simplified form)

马 马字旁
Mǎzi páng

乛 马 马   马

mǎ, *horse*

丶 口 口 叮 吅 吅 呎 骂 骂   骂

mà, *to scold*

The earth radical

 提土旁
Tí tǔ páng

一 十 土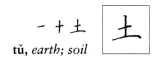
tǔ, *earth; soil*

一 十 土 切 地 地 地
dì, *the ground; place*

The fire radical

 火字旁
Huǒzi páng

丶 丷 少 火 火
huǒ, *fire*

丶 丷 少 火 火 灯 灯 炒 炒
chǎo, *to stir-fry, to fry*

The jade radical

Wángzi páng

This element is called the *king radical* in Chinese, and it looks like the character for *king* when it appears as a radical:

王   wáng, *king*   一 二 干 王

The character for *jade* is written by adding a dot—a jade ornament—to the king, like this:

玉   yù, *jade*   一 二 干 王 玉

When *jade* appears as a radical, the dot is eliminated, but the radical appears in many characters that denote valuable or beautiful things, revealing its true heritage.

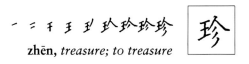

zhēn, *treasure; to treasure*

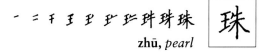

zhū, *pearl*

The tree radical

Mùzi páng

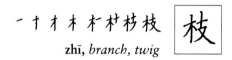 
mù, *tree; wood*

一 十 才 木 木 杧 枝 枝
zhī, *branch, twig*

The carriage radical (full form)

Chēzi páng

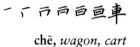
chē, *wagon, cart*

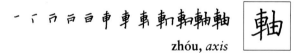
zhóu, *axis*

The carriage radical (simplified form)

车字旁
Chēzi páng

一 七 圥 车
chē, *wagon, cart*
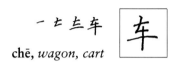

一 七 车 车 轫 轫 轫 轴 轴
zhóu, *axis*

The sun radical

日字旁
Rìzi páng

丨 冂 冃 日
rì, *sun; day*
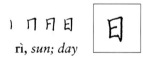

丨 冂 日 日 刖 明 明 明
míng, *light, bright*

The meat radical

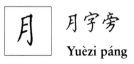

月字旁
Yuèzi páng

Like the jade radical above, the meat radical looks like something other than it is—in this case, **yuè**, *moon:*

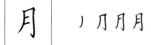

It is therefore called the moon radical in Chinese. Actually, it is usually a shortened form of **ròu**, *meat:*

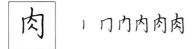

It appears in many characters that have to do with the body.

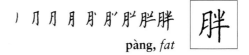

pàng, *fat*

The cowrie radical (full form)

Bèizi páng

Cowrie shells were used as money in ancient China, so this radical appears in many characters that denote valuable things or that have to do with trade and business.

丨 刂 冂 冃 目 目 目 貝　**貝**

bèi, *shell; cowrie*

丨 冂 冃 冃 目 貝 貝 貝 貝 貝 貝 貯 購 購 購 購　**購**

gòu, *to buy*

The cowrie radical (simplified form)

贝　贝字旁
Bèizi páng

丨 冂 贝 贝　**贝**

bèi, *shell; cowrie*

丨 冂 贝 贝 贝 贩 购 购　**购**

gòu, *to buy*

The sickness radical

疒　病字旁
Bìngzi páng

丶 亠 广 广 疒 疒 疒 病 病 病　**病**

bìng, *sick*

The eye radical

目字旁
Mùzi páng

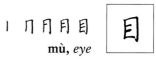

丨 冂 冃 月 目
mù, *eye*

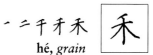

ノ 二 三 手 尹 看 看 看 看
kàn, *to look*

The grain radical

禾字旁
Hézi páng

禾
丿 二 千 禾 禾
hé, *grain*

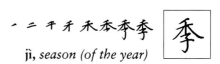

科
丿 二 千 禾 禾 禾 禾 科 科
kē, *department*

季
丿 二 千 禾 禾 季 季 季
jì, *season (of the year)*

The bamboo radical

竹字头
Zhúzi tóu

丿 ㇒ ㇏ ㇒ 竹 竹
zhú, *bamboo*
竹

丿 ㇒ ㇏ ㇒ 竹 竹 ㇒ 竺 竺 笁 箣 筆
bǐ, *pen; (writing) brush* (full form)
筆

丿 ㇒ ㇏ ㇒ 竹 竹 ㇒ 竺 竺 笔
bǐ, *pen; (writing) brush* (simplified form)
笔

The foot radical

足字旁
Zúzi páng

丶 ㇇ 口 甼 甼 品 足
zú, *foot*
足

丶 ㇇ 口 甼 甼 品 足 趵 趵 趵 跳 跳 跳
tiào, *to jump*
跳

The rain radical

 雨字头
Yǔzi tóu

一 厂 厂 雨 雨 雨 雨 雨
yǔ, *rain*

一 厂 厂 雨 雨 雨 雨 雨 雪 雪 雪 雷 雷
léi, *thunder*

一 厂 厂 雨 雨 雨 雨 雪 雪 雪 雪
xuě, *snow*

The metal radical (full form)

 金字旁
Jīnzi páng

丿 人 人 全 全 余 余 金
jīn, *gold*

丿 人 人 今 今 令 余 金 金 錢 錢 錢 錢 錢 錢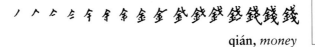
qián, *money*

The metal radical (simplified form)

金字旁
Jīnzi páng

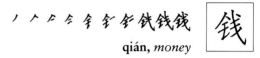

qián, *money*

The altar-stand radical

示字旁
Shìzi páng

It is easy to mix this radical up with the next radical, the *clothing* radical, for they differ by only one dot. But if you compare the characters from which they are derived, **shì,** *to show,* and **yī,** *clothing,* any confusion will vanish. The characters in which the two radicals appear also give them away.

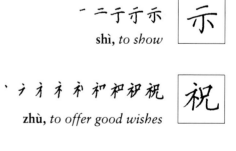

shì, *to show*

zhù, *to offer good wishes*

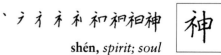

shén, *spirit; soul*

The clothing radical

 补衣旁
Bǔ yī páng

丶 亠 亣 亣 衣 衣
yī, clothing

丶 亠 亣 亣 衣 衤 初 衻 袨 被 被
bèi, *quilt*

丶 亠 亣 亣 衣 衤 初 衻 袖 袖
xiù, *sleeve*

The dog radical

 反犬旁
Fǎn quǎn páng

丿 犭 犭 犭 犳 狗 狗 狗
gǒu, *dog*

丿 犭 犭 犭 犳 犳 狠 狼 狼
láng, *wolf*

A POEM AND MORE CHARACTERS

TO PRACTICE

The nonnative student of Chinese needs to master the most common characters first. Below I list a hundred or so common Chinese characters that have not been mentioned earlier. They were chosen mainly for their frequency of occurrence in everyday language; the most frequent are listed first. Both full and simplified variants have been included. Those common characters that have appeared as examples in the text are not repeated here.

The traditional way of practicing calligraphy has always been to copy classical poems. It is important to sometimes write whole texts, for characters are not only entities in themselves but parts of a whole; each must harmonize with the rest on a page of text. When you write **kǎishū**, all characters should be uniform in size, and the **héng** strokes of different characters should have a similar slant and curvature. Before moving on to the exercises, let us practice characters in context. Later you will undoubtedly want to copy poems and scrolls on your own to perfect your handwriting in Chinese.

"A Thought on a Still Night"

The **Táng**-dynasty poem presented here is meant as a traditional exercise. By writing it, you can practice calligraphy and, as a bonus, glimpse the poetry of this golden age. The poem was composed by **Lǐ Bái**, perhaps the most famous poet of the time. **Lǐ** was born in 699 and died in 762. It is said that he

Fig. 18. Poem with simplified characters

Fig. 19. Poem with full characters

was very lazy as a child. One day, however, while out walking he met an old woman sitting by the road. She was holding a thick iron rod on which she worked with a file. When young Lǐ asked what she was doing, she answered, "I am making a sewing needle." After that day Lǐ Bái became more industrious in his schoolwork.

I have chosen his poem **Jìng yè sī** because it contains only rather common characters. It appears with simplified characters in figure 18 and with full characters in figure 19.

The place, date, and signature of the calligrapher are usually written to the left of the poem. The signature is followed by the character **shū**, which in classical Chinese means *to write*, and by the seal of the calligrapher. Sometimes the title or original author of the poem are also added here. Making attractive frames like the ones in the figures, writing the characters, and signing your works in the traditional way can be fun and rewarding; it is not hard to make frames if you have a ruler and a pen that draws lines of even thickness.

> **Jìng yè sī**
>
> **chuáng qián míng yuè guāng**
> **yí shì dì shàng shuāng**
> **jǔ tóu wàng míng yuè**
> **dī tóu sī gù xiāng**

Here are the strokes for those characters in the poem that have not appeared earlier in the book.

jìng, *still, quiet*

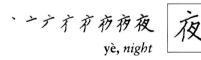

yè, *night*

ㄴ ㄐ ㄐ ㄐ ㄐ- ㄐ† ㄐ† ㄐ††　牀

chuáng, *bed* (full form)

、 ㄧ 广 广 庐 床 床　床

chuáng, *bed* (simplified form)

、 ㄨ ㅄ 广 芦 芾 首 前 前　前

qián, *before; in front of*

ノ 丬 ㅄ 屮 屮 光　光

guāng, *light*

ㅌ ㄷ ㄷ ㄷ ㅌ 妄 矣 矣 疑 疑 疑 疑 疑　疑

yí, *to suspect; to think*

一 卜 上　上

shàng, *upon; up; above*

、 ㄧ 雨 雨 雨 雨 霏 霏 霏 霜 霜 霜 霜　霜

shuāng, *frost*

ノ ㄈ ㄈ ㄈ ㄈ 肸 肸 陟 陟 舁 與 與 與 與 舉 舉 舉　舉

jǔ, *to lift, to raise* (full form)

举

jǔ, *to lift, to raise* (simplified form)

頭

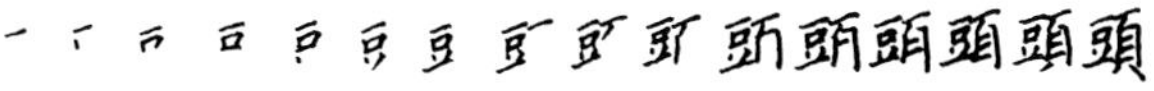

tóu, *head* (full form)

头

tóu, *head* (simplified form)

望

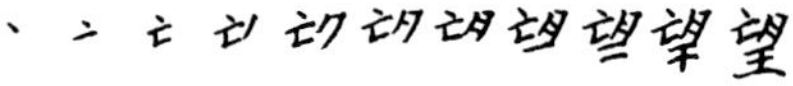

wàng, *to regard, to look at*

地

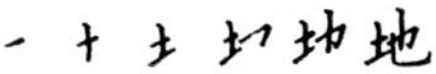

dī, *low; to lower*

故

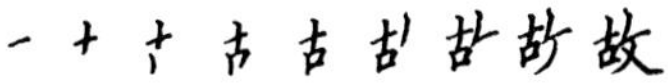

gù, *old; former*

鄉

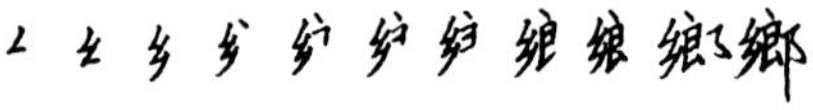

xiāng, *countryside* (full form)

乡

xiāng, *countryside* (simplifed form)

Remember that, in a Chinese sentence, place words like *on* and *in front of* come after that which they locate; thus, for example, "ground upon frost" means *frost upon (the) ground*. The poem then becomes easy to understand.

Still night thought

bed front bright moon light
[one might] think is ground upon frost
raise head regard bright moon
lower head think old home

A smoother translation might go like this:

A Thought on a Still Night

Before my bed the bright moonlight
Looks like frost upon the ground.
I raise my head to watch the moon,
Then lower my head and think of home.

Characters to Practice

ノ 亻 亇 亇 自 的 的 的   的
de, *a grammatical particle*

⁀ 了   了
le, *a grammatical particle*

丶 冂 冂 四 四   四
sì, *four*

一 丁 丆 五   五
wǔ, *five*

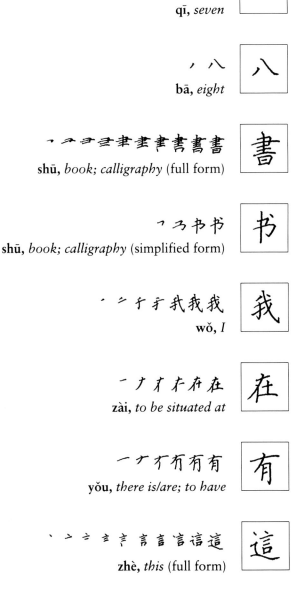

一 乇
qī, *seven*

丿 八
bā, *eight*

フ フ ユ ヨ ヨ 聿 聿 書 書 書 書
shū, *book; calligraphy* (full form)

フ 乃 书 书
shū, *book; calligraphy* (simplified form)

丿 二 千 于 我 我 我
wǒ, *I*

一 ナ 才 才 在 在
zài, *to be situated at*

一 ナ 才 有 有 有
yǒu, *there is/are; to have*

丶 亠 ㇒ 亖 言 言 言 言 语 这
zhè, *this* (full form)

、 亠 文 文 这 这 **这**

zhè, *this* (simplified form)

ノ 亻 仴 仴 仴 侢 侢 們 們 們 **們**

men, *a grammatical particle* (full form)

ノ 亻 亣 亣 们 **们**

men, *a grammatical particle* (simplified form)

ノ 亻 亻 们 們 們 個 個 個 個 **個**

ge, *a classifier* (full form)

ノ 人 个 **个**

ge, *a classifier* (simplified form)

、 丷 丷 兰 兰 芊 荠 荠 着 着 着 **着**

zhe or **zháo,** *a grammatical particle*

ノ 亻 千 仴 仴 臼 臼 兒 **兒**

ér, *son* (full form)

ノ 儿 **儿**

ér, *son* (simplified form)

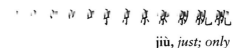 就
jiù, *just; only*

一 エ 工 巧 耳 至 到 到 到
dào, *to arrive*

フ 了 子
zǐ, *son*

´ ⺅ 彳 彳 彳 彳 彳 彳 得 得
de, *a grammatical particle*, or **děi**, *must; to have to*

一 十 土 去 去
qù, *to go*

フ ヲ ヨ 月 那 那
nà, *that*

 會
huì, *can; to know how to* (full form)

ノ 人 人 仐 仐 会 会
huì, *can; to know how to* (simplified form)

、 ー 二 宇 主　主
zhǔ, *main*

丶 冂 日 日 日- 旷 旷 旷 時 時　時
shí, *time* (full form)

丶 冂 日 日 日- 时 时　时
shí, *time* (simplified form)

𠃊 𠃊 中 出 出　出
chū, *out; to come out*

丨 冂 冋 冋 丹 丹 咼 咼 渦 渦 過　過
guò, *to pass* (full form)

一 寸 寸 寸 讨 过　过
guò, *to pass* (simplified form)

丶 丿 𠂇 为 为 为 为 为 为　為
wéi, lit., *to be, to function as,* or **wèi,** *for* (full form)

丶 丿 力 为　为
wéi, lit., *to be, to function as,* or **wèi,** *for* (simplified form)

ノ イ 亻 仕 什 估 估 佴 做 做 做 做
zuò, *to do* 做

ノ 亻 门 门 自 自
zì, *self* 自

ノ ヲ ヺ 癶 癶 癶 癶 癶 發 發 發 發
fā, *to emit; to become* (full form) 發

レ ⺿ 发 发 发
fā, *to emit; to become* (simplified form) 发

フ 又
yòu, *once more, again* 又

一 丁 丆 丙 而 而 而 面 面
miàn, *face; surface* 面

一 十 才 才 木 机 相 相 相 相 想 想 想 想
xiǎng, *to think* 想

一 十 才 才 木 术 杙 杙 栏 栏 样 样 样 様 様
yàng, *kind, sort* (full form) 様

一 十 才 木 术 术 术 栏 栏 样

yàng, *kind, sort* (simplified form) 样

丶 丷 丷 兰 羊 生 羊 差 羊 羡 義 義 義

yì, *righteous; meaning* (full form) 義

丶 丿 义

yì, *righteous; meaning* (simplified form) 义

丿 彳 彳 衤 衼 衼 後 後 後

hòu, *after* (full form) 後

一 厂 广 斤 后 后

hòu, *after* (simplified form) 后

く 幺 女 如 如 她

tā, *she* 她

幺 幺 幺 纟 糹 糹 紅 紂 經 經 經 經 經

jīng, *via; past* (full form) 經

幺 幺 纟 纟 织 经 绍 经

jīng, *via; past* (simplified form) 经

產

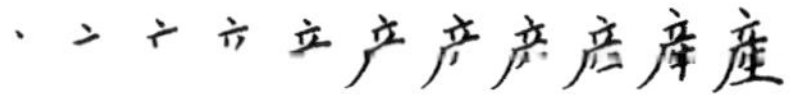

chǎn, *to produce* (full form)

产

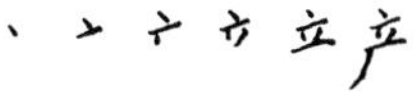

chǎn, *to produce* (simplified form)

然

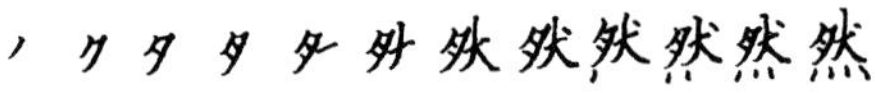

rán, *in this way*

種

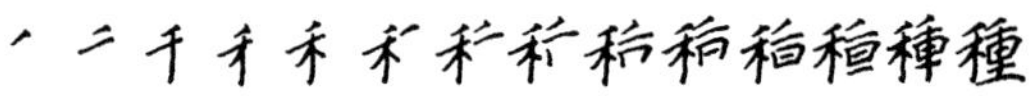

zhǒng, *sort, kind,* or **zhòng,** *to plant, to grow* (full form)

种

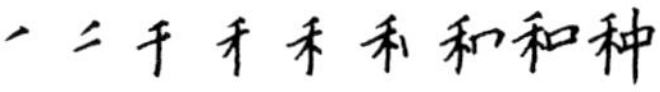

zhǒng, *sort, kind,* or **zhòng,** *to plant, to grow* (simplified form)

老

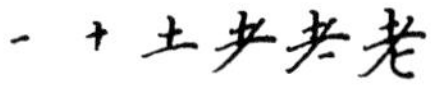

lǎo, *old*

事

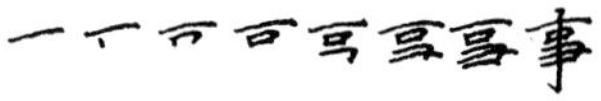

shì, *matter, business*

從

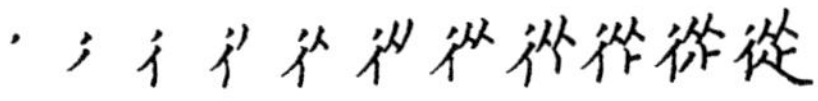

cóng, *from* (full form)

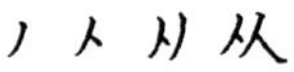

从

cóng, *from* (simplified form)

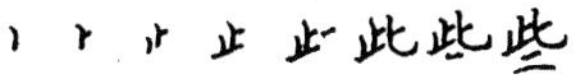

些

xiē, *some*

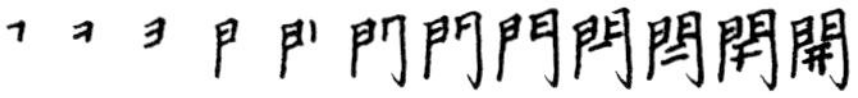

開

kāi, *to open* (full form)

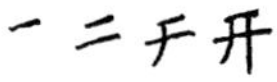

开

kāi, *to open* (simplified form)

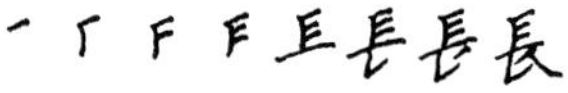

長

cháng, *long,* or **zhǎng,** *to grow* (full form)

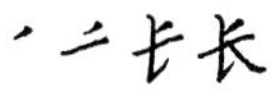

长

cháng, *long,* or **zhǎng,** *to grow* (simplified form)

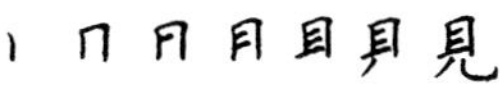

見

jiàn, *to see* (full form)

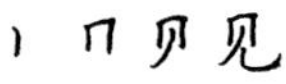

见

jiàn, *to see* (simplified form)

一 十 土 キ キ 走 走　走

zǒu, *to walk*

丶 亠 六 古 古 高 高 高 高　高

gāo, *high, tall*

丶 丷 宀 宀 宇 宇 宇 宇 宇 宇 宇 宇 實 實　實

shí, *real* (full form)

丶 丷 宀 宀 宀 空 空 实 实　实

shí, *real* (simplified form)

丿 一 丘 气 气 气 氧 氧 氣　氣

qì, *air* (full form)

丿 一 丘 气　气

qì, *air* (simplified form)

丶 丷 宀 宀 它　它

tā, *it*

ㄥ ㄠ ㄠ ㄠ 糸 糸 糸 糸 糸 糸 給 給 給　給

gěi, *to give* (full form)

ㄥ 幺 ㄠ 纟 纩 绘 纷 给 给
gěi, *to give* (simplified form)

＾ ニ 三 手
shǒu, *hand*

ノ 人 人 人 全 全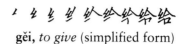
quán, *whole; fully*

フ 力
lì, *force*

一 丁 下 正 正
zhèng, *straight; proper; front*

丶 宀 宀 宁 宇 定 定
dìng, *to order; to decide*

丶 亠 ゙ 亠 立 产 产 音 音 意 意
yì, *meaning*

一 十 才 木 朮 朳 朳 桦 楲 楲 楲 機 機 機
jī, *machine; opportunity* (full form)

一 十 才 木 利 机
jī, *machine; opportunity* (simplified form)

丶 亻 冂 向 向 向
xiàng, *in the direction of*

丶 冂 口 ロ 吅 叩 吅 畕 罝 單 罩 單 戰 戰 戰
zhàn, *war* (full form)

一 卜 ⺊ 占 占 占 战 战 战
zhàn, *war* (simplified form)

丶 ⺊ 牛 牛 牜 物 物 物
wù, *object, thing*

一 二 Ŧ 王 玝 玾 珇 珇 理 理 理
lǐ, *to order, to straighten out; logic*

一 十 士 吉 吉 吉 声 声 殸 殸 殸 殼 殼 殸 聲 聲 聲
shēng, *sound, noise* (full form)

一 十 士 吉 吉 吉 声
shēng, *sound, noise* (simplified form)

, 一 ∠ 灬 灬 灬 灬 笁 笁 等 等　**等**
děng, *to wait*

丨 冂 内 内　**内**
nèi, *inside*

ノ ク タ 列 外　**外**
wài, *outside*

丶 冫 氵 氵 汁 浐 法 法　**法**
fǎ, *law; method*

ノ イ 仁 化　**化**
huà, *change*

丶 丶 忄 忄 忄 怊 情 情 情 情　**情**
qíng, *feeling*

丨 冂 月 月 目 目 即 肥 眼 眼 眼　**眼**
yǎn, *eye*

丶 丿 亻 勺 勺 自 身 身　**身**
shēn, *body*

ノ 厂 厉 反

fǎn, *opposite, anti-*

一 丁 丌 且 且 且 耳 耳 耳 耵 聊 聊 聍 聍 聴 聴 聽 聽 聽

tīng, *to hear; to listen* (full form)

丶 丷 口 口 叮 听 听

tīng, *to hear; to listen* (simplified form)

丶 口 日 日 旦 早 异 昌 昌 昌 最 最

zuì, *most*

一 厂 广 币 币 币 币 零 零 零 雪 雷 電

diàn, *lightning; electricity* (full form)

丶 口 口 日 电

diàn, *lightning; electricity* (simplified form)

丶 亠 亠 六 立 立 辛 辛 亲 亲 新 新 新

xīn, *new*

ノ ク ゲ 夕 角 角 角 解 解 解 解 解 解

jiě, *to solve*

丨 丿 小 少

shǎo, *little, few*

丨 凵 山

shān, *mountain*

丨 亅 彐 𦣻 𠃌 門 門 門 門 閂 閂 閂 閂 關 關 關 關 關

guān, *to close* (full form)

丶 丷 丷 䒑 关 关

guān, *to close* (simplified form)

丿 几 凡 凡 凬 凬 風 風 風

fēng, *wind* (full form)

丿 几 凡 风

fēng, *wind* (simplified form)

丶 口 口 𤴓 𤴓 足 足 𧾷 趴 趵 跟 跟 跟

gēn, *with, together with*

丶 二 亠 六 立 立 辛 亲 亲 亲 𣐃 𣐃 𣐃 親 親

qīn, *relatives* (full form)

、 ㇗ 立 产 辛 亲 亲

qīn, *relatives* (simplified form)

ノ ト x ㇙ ㄠ ㄊ 灶 竺 竺 笑 笑

xiào, *to laugh*

ノ ㇇ ㄅ ㄅ ㄅ 色

sè, *color*

SUGGESTED READINGS

Should you want to delve further into the subjects discussed in this book, you will find food for thought in the books listed here.

China—Empire of Living Symbols by Cecilia Lindqvist. A modern classic on the historical development of the characters, translated from the Swedish original, which was published in 1989. (London: Harville HarperCollins, 1991; Reading, Mass.: Addison-Wesley, 1991.)

Chinese Calligraphers and Their Art by Ch'en Chih-Mai. A thorough discussion of the history of calligraphy with in-depth portraits of some of the great masters. The author also deals with aesthetics and appreciation of calligraphy, but gives little practical guidance on writing and does not analyze individual characters. (London and New York: Cambridge University Press, 1966.)

Chinese Calligraphy by Lucy Driscoll and Kenji Toda. A brilliant exposition of calligraphy as an art form. (Chicago: University of Chicago Press, 1935.)

Chinese Calligraphy: An Introduction to Its Aesthetic and Technique by Chiang Yee. A comprehensive and frequently amusing introduction to the history, aesthetics, and practice of calligraphy, written by an old-fashioned Chinese scholar. The examples tend to include very obscure characters. (3rd ed. Cambridge: Harvard University Press, 1973.)

A multitude of books and character patterns are available in larger Chinese bookshops. The editions are quickly sold out, making it pointless to give any particular titles. Have a look at what is currently on the shelves.

Pīnyīn is a standard system of writing Chinese using the Latin alphabet.

Consonants

The consonants **f, h, m, n, ng, r, s,** and **sh** are pronounced as in English. The *ch* in the English word *cheek* sounds like a *t* followed by a soft *sh*-like sound; the Chinese **x** is pronounced like this soft *sh*.

The consonant **l** is similar to an upper-class British one—"An absolutely *splendid* party, my dear chap!"—as opposed to a cockney *l* or a thick American Midwestern one.

A number of Chinese sounds form unaspirated-aspirated pairs. We say a sound is aspirated when it is accompanied by a puff of air, like the English *t* in *town*. Say the word holding the palm of your hand close to your mouth— you should feel the *t* coming out. The unaspirated form of *t* is *d*—if you say *down* you can't feel the *d* against your palm. In English *d* is voiced—the vocal cords vibrate when you say it—so *d* and *t* differ by both voicing and aspiration. In Chinese **d** is unvoiced, just like the **t,** so the only difference between **d** and **t** is the aspiration. The unaspirated-aspirated pairs in Chinese are the following:

b-p pronounced as in English, but **b** is unvoiced

d-t pronounced as in English, but **d** is unvoiced

g-k pronounced as in English, but **g** is unvoiced

j-q **j** is pronounced as in *job,* **q** like *tch* in *kitchen*

z-c pronounced like the English *ds* and a *ts,* respectively, but the *ds* is unvoiced

zh-ch **zh** is pronounced like *dr* in *draw;* **ch** is more aspirated than the English *ch*

Vowels and Diphthongs

The letter **a** is usually pronounced like the *u* in *fun;* **ian,** however, is pronounced like *yen.*

The letter **e** is usually pronounced like the *ea* in *learn;* however, in the combinations **ei** and **ie** it is pronounced like the English *a* in *lay.*

The letter **i** is pronounced in three different ways: after **r, sh, zh,** and **ch** it sounds like an *r,* so **shi** is pronounced like *shr,* **ri** like *rr,* and so on. After **s, z,** and **c** it is pronounced like the *z* sound in *buzz;* **si** sounds like *szz,* **zi** like *dzz,* and **ci** like *tzz.* In all other cases **i** is pronounced like the *e* in *she.*

The letter **o** is usually pronounced like *aw* in *saw;* in **ong,** however, it is pronounced like *oo* in *soon.*

The letter **ü** is pronounced like the *y* at the beginning of English words. The word *you,* for example, is made up of a short, soft *y* sound followed by an *oo: yoo.* The Chinese **ü** sounds like this *y.*

The letter **u** is usually pronounced like *oo* in *soon;* after **j, q, x,** and **y,** however, it is pronounced like **ü.**

The diphthong **ou** is pronounced like *o* in *go.*

The Chinese **y** is silent and is used in **pīnyīn** for historical reasons. Thus, for example, **yi** is pronounced like a lone **i,** or *ee,* and **yu** is pronounced like **ü.** Similarly, the **u**-sound is spelled **w** when it occurs in an initial position; for example, **wu** is pronounced *oo.*

Tones

There are four tones in Chinese, indicated here with diacritics.

- ā The first tone is level, like the tone of the second syllable of *tadaa!* Someone whisking the drape off a new painting or announcing, with a flourish, the opening of a school play might say *tadaa!*

- á The second tone is rising, like the tone of a surprised question: *What?*

- ǎ The third tone goes down and then up, just like the irritated and somewhat exaggerated tone used on *so* in the following context: *"You haven't given me any reason to do it." "So? Do it anyway."*

- à The fourth tone is a falling tone that sounds like the tone on *hey* in *"Hey! You there!"*

INDEX OF CHARACTERS

All characters used as examples and exercises in the text and for which a stroke order has been included are listed below.

diàn, *shop*, 66
dìng, *to order; to decide*, 107
dòng, *to move; to touch*, 101
dōu, *all, every*, 100
duì, *correct, right*, 101
duō, *much, more than*, 101

ér, *a grammatical particle*, 60
ér, *son*, 97
èr, *two*, 33

fā, *to emit; to become*, 102
fǎ, *law; method*, 109
fǎn, *opposite, anti-*, 110
fàn, *rice; food*, 74
fāng, *place, location*, 49
fēng, *wind*, 111
fù, *high place, mound*, 68

gāo, *high, tall*, 106
ge, *a classifier*, 97
gěi, *to give*, 106
gēn, *with, together with*, 111
gōng, *work*, 101
gǒu, *dog*, 89
gòu, *to buy*, 84
gù, *old; former*, 94
guān, *to close*, 111
guǎng, *broad, wide*, 66
guó, *country*, 42, 48, 54
guò, *to pass*, 99

hái, *still; yet*, 100
hán, *letter, epistle*, 47
háng, *row, line*, 67
hǎo, *good*, 47
hé, *grain*, 85
hé, *river*, 39
hēi, *black*, 39
hěn, *very, to a high degree*, 67

hóng, *red*, 37, 56
hòu, *after*, 103
huā, *flower*, 73
huà, *change*, 109
huí, *to return*, 54
huì, *can; to know how to*, 98
huǒ, *fire*, 35, 79

jī, *machine, opportunity*, 107
jí, *impatient; worried*, 70
jí, *to reach, to attain*, 45
jì, *season (of the year)*, 85
jiā, *home, family*, 65
jiàn, *to see*, 105
jiào, *to call; to call for*, 74
jiē, *street*, 58
jiě, *to solve*, 110
jīn, *gold*, 87
jìn, *close, nearby*, 36
jìn, *to enter, to go in*, 72
jīng, *capital city*, 64
jīng, *via; past*, 103
jìng, *still, quiet*, 92
jiǔ, *nine*, 43
jiù, *just; only*, 98
jǔ, *to lift, to raise*, 93
jù, *sentence*, 47

kāi, *to open*, 105
kàn, *to look*, 85
kē, *department*, 85
kě, *but*, 59
kǒu, *mouth; opening*, 74

láng, *wolf*, 89
lǎo, *old*, 104
le, *a grammatical particle*, 95
léi, *thunder*, 87
lǐ, *to order, to straighten out; logic*, 108
lì, *force*, 107